# BREAKFAST GROUP

THE

## at the Carl Cherry Center for the Arts

November 1- December 15, 2013

# THE BREAKFAST GROUP

The Breakfast Group -
a half century of java and jive
on the Road to Carmel

The Breakfast Group was born in the Sixties of a group of artists teaching at the University of California at Berkeley who began meeting every week to discuss art, teaching, and individual pursuits. As coffee flowed, so did conversation extending to film and politics and, naturally, sports.

The Breakfast Group takes to the Road to come to the Carl Cherry Center for the Arts bringing a mix of art and artists. This exhibition of work provides a taste of current art in the Bay Area: painting and drawing - abstraction and figuration, photography and computer art, sculpture and three dimensional printing. With work rooted in many traditions and diverging along individual paths, the members of the Breakfast Group represent a broad perspective.

It is not a stylistic unity, nor is it a material commonality which binds these artists. They work with paint on canvas, they work with steel or glass, and they even work on computers. What they do share, that from which they all partake, is an interest in the work around them, an engagement in the dialogue of contemporary art, and an open and questioning relationship to the world and current events.

At the core of this association has been the importance of mutual support and encouragement. From diverse artistic practices and philosophical perspectives, the members of the Breakfast Group have a shared sense of purpose as artists in a complex relationship to contemporary society.

Though the time and location has shifted over the years, though the membership has included different voices, and even though some of the early members only attend when stories told and retold evoke their presence, the spirit of the Breakfast Group remains deeply rooted in fertile ground.

A cup of java may not be 10 cents any more, but the flow of camaraderie from that cup has not diminished. The Breakfast Group is very happy to imbibe in Carmel and to share morning musings with new found friends. The Breakfast Group comes bringing stories, announcements and catalogues from shows they have seen, shows they have been in, or just the morning art section from the New York Times. Sitting down to breakfast in the Cherry Center, seeing the artwork in the light and calm of Carmel, starting a new conversation with members of the Carmel community, a fresh dialogue opens.

-Jan Wurm

# at the Carl Cherry Center for the Arts

## WHY YOU SHOULD ALWAYS EAT YOUR BREAKFAST

Breakfast is the most important meal of the day – and perhaps the most energetic. Even now, after nearly half a century, *The Breakfast Group* continues to reflect the visual exuberance and verve of the East Bay's seminal art community. Meeting each Friday morning, in what had begun as a weekly lunch and then morphed into breakfast so that it would not break up the painting day, Elmer Bischoff and Sidney Gordon were joined by Erle Loran, Hassel Smith, George Lloyd, and Jerry Carlin. This informal assembly of artists would gather over wheat toast, scrambled eggs, grapefruit juice and coffee to express their artistic concerns or to simply talk about the Forty Niners, the Cal teams and the day's news.

At the same time there has never been anything remotely organized about the *Breakfast Group*, nothing resembling a *Breakfast Group* art association -- let alone a Breakfast Movement in the way there was a Bay Area Figurative Movement. There was simply a loose coalition of artists, friends, University of California faculty members, colleagues and artistic neighbors, who sometimes painted together--or not.

As a result there are few common denominators that characterize the art. No sign posts or schools. In this way, the impulsive, fleeting nature of the East Bay provides a likely starting point for an inquiry into its art and artists. Far from being an inclusive view, the art of *The Breakfast Group* is as reflective and varied as the setting from which it materializes. Many of the pieces in the current exhibit are engaging and beautifully rendered, but what engenders them most valuable is a special kind of integrity in their presentation of "art." The unambiguously dynamic art of *The Breakfast Group* makes a point for the vitality and resolve of art made in the San Francisco Bay Area.

--- Robert Reese
the Carl Cherry Center for the Arts

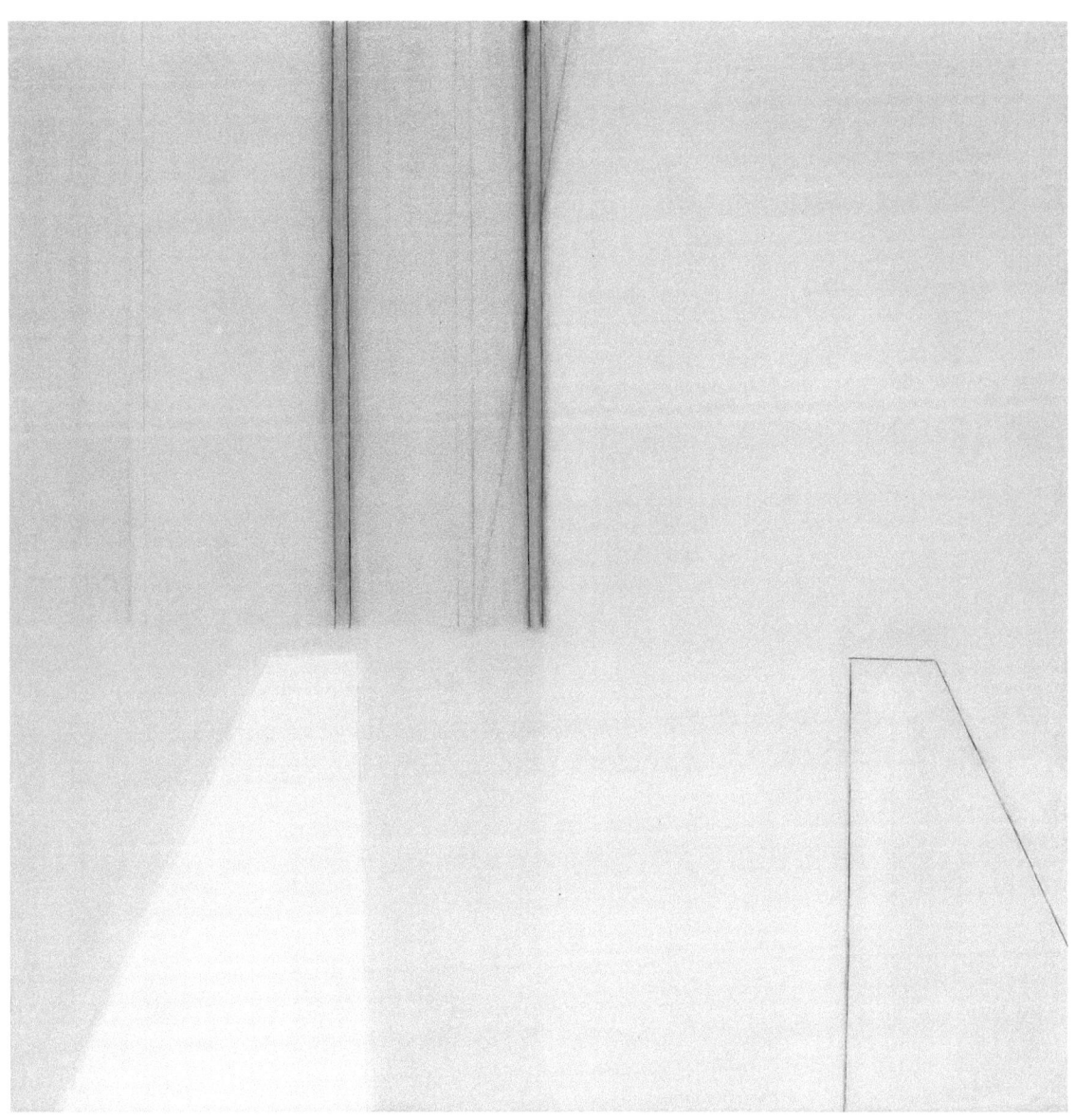

Edythe Bresnahan  Siena Series #78  16″x16″  Oil on panel  2012

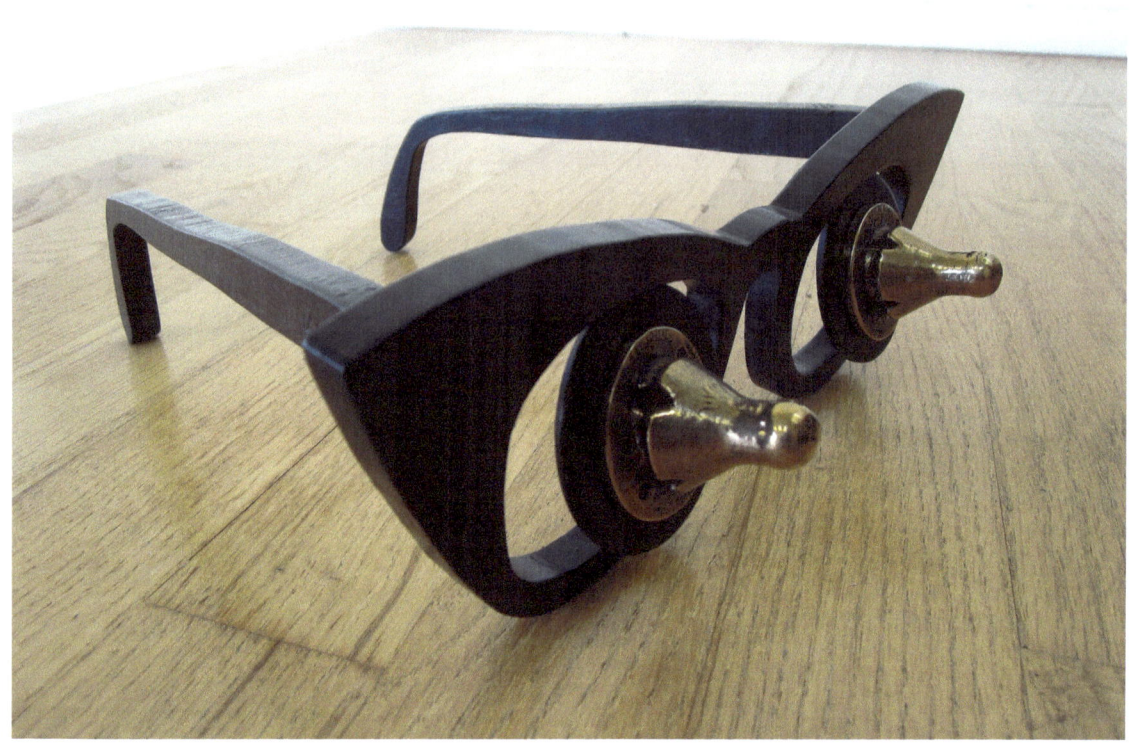

Bruce Chaban  Magnet  10″(h)x8″(l)x3″(h)  Steel and bronze  2012

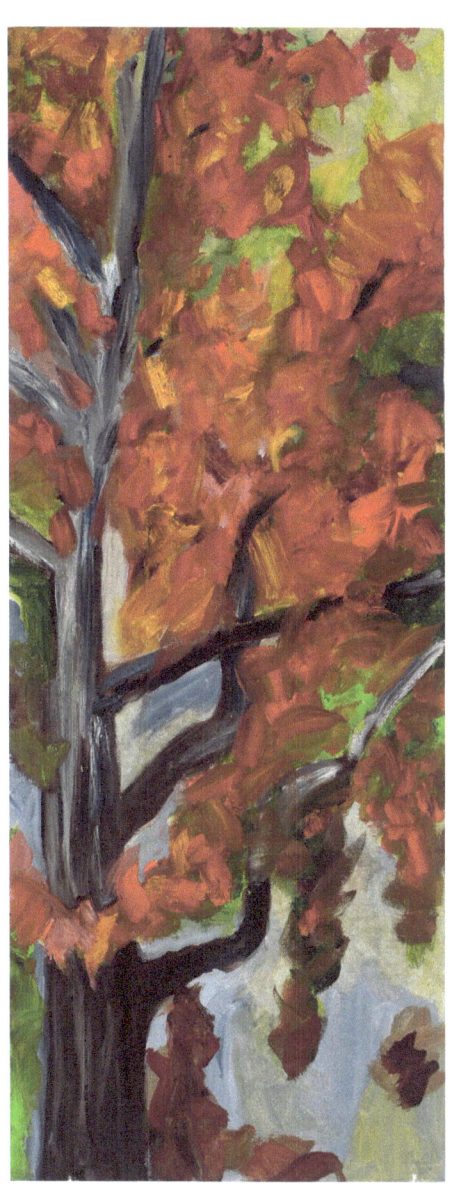

Donna Fenstermaker  12.28.12  MVC  30″x12″  Oil on canvas  2012

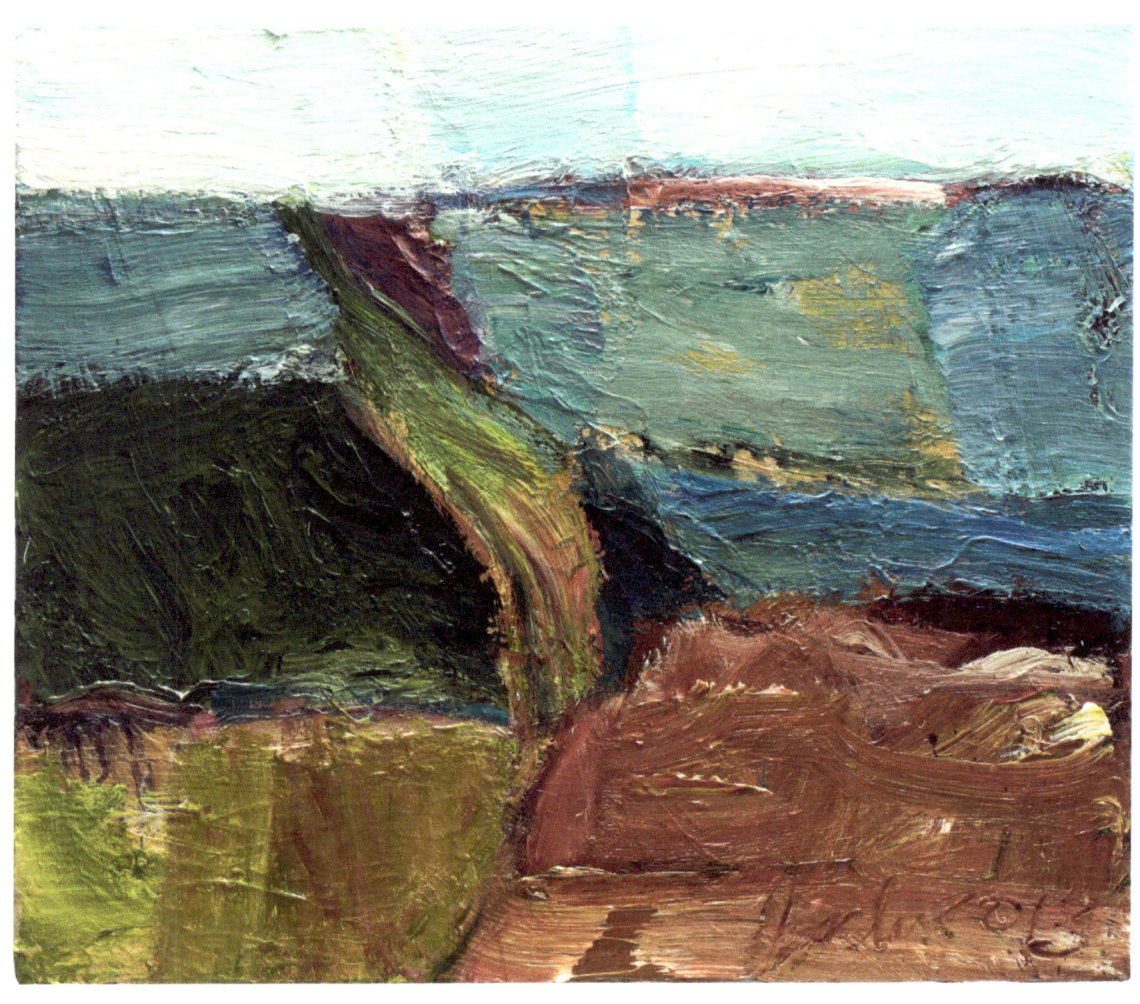

Lin Fischer  The Road is Long 11 20″x24″  Acrylic on canvas  2013

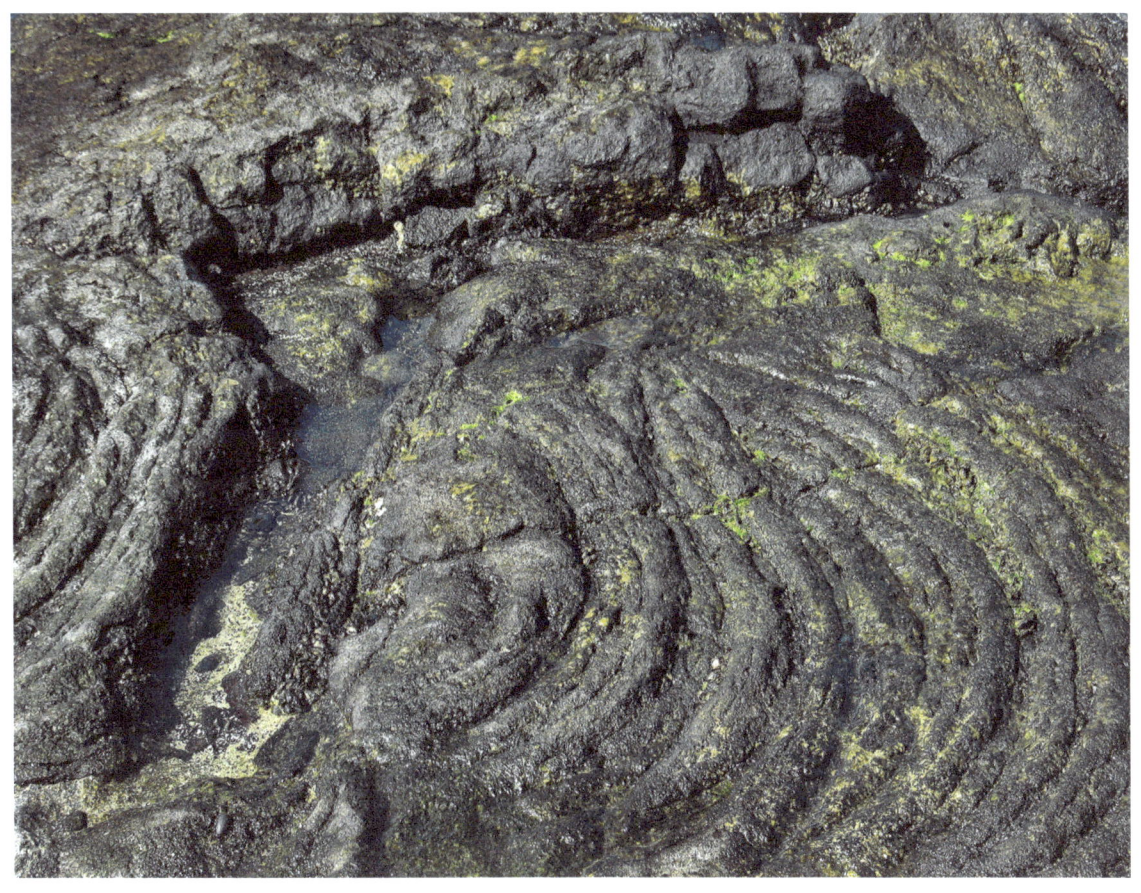

John Friedman  Lava Tidepool - Hawaii Island  18″x22″  Photograph, archival dye print 2009/2013

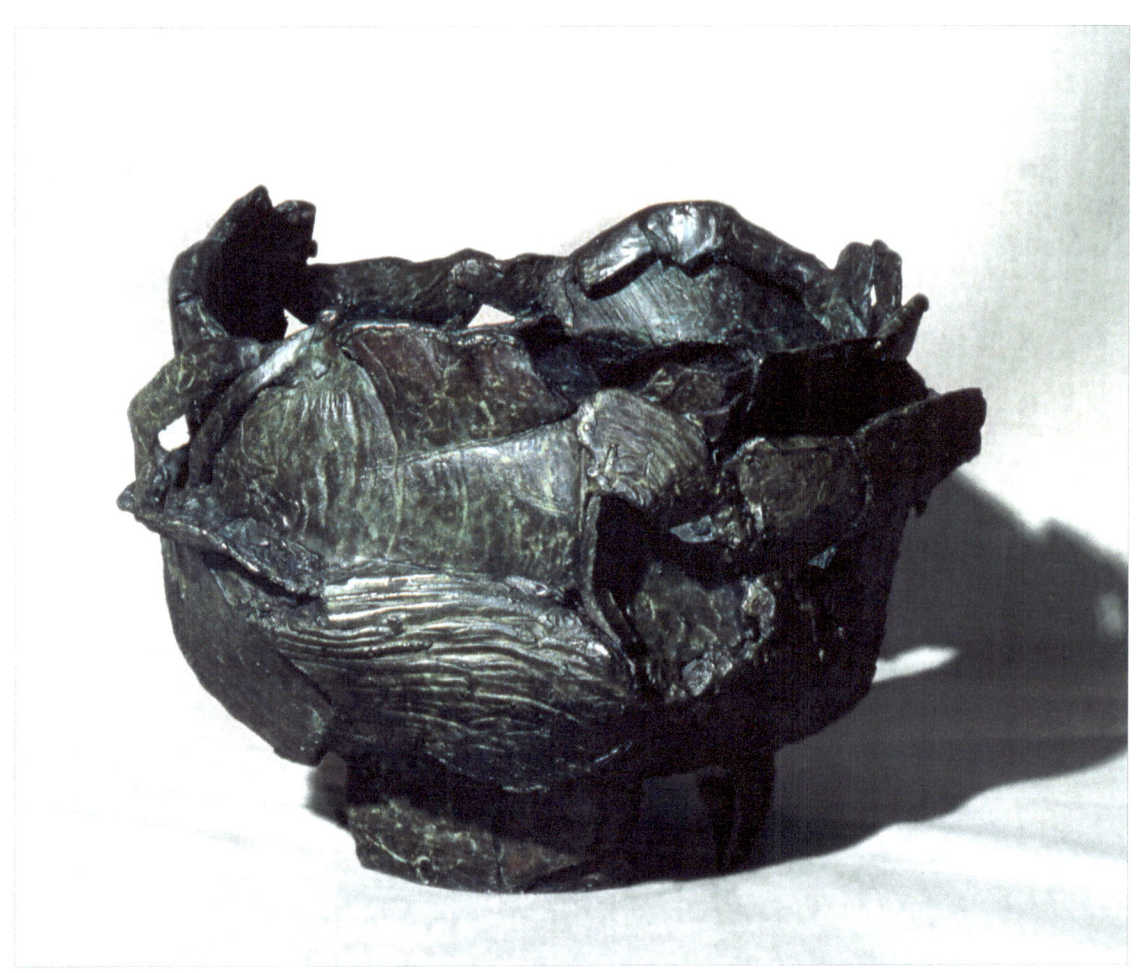

Nancy Genn  Vessel: Wave  11″x11″x15″  Bronze  2009

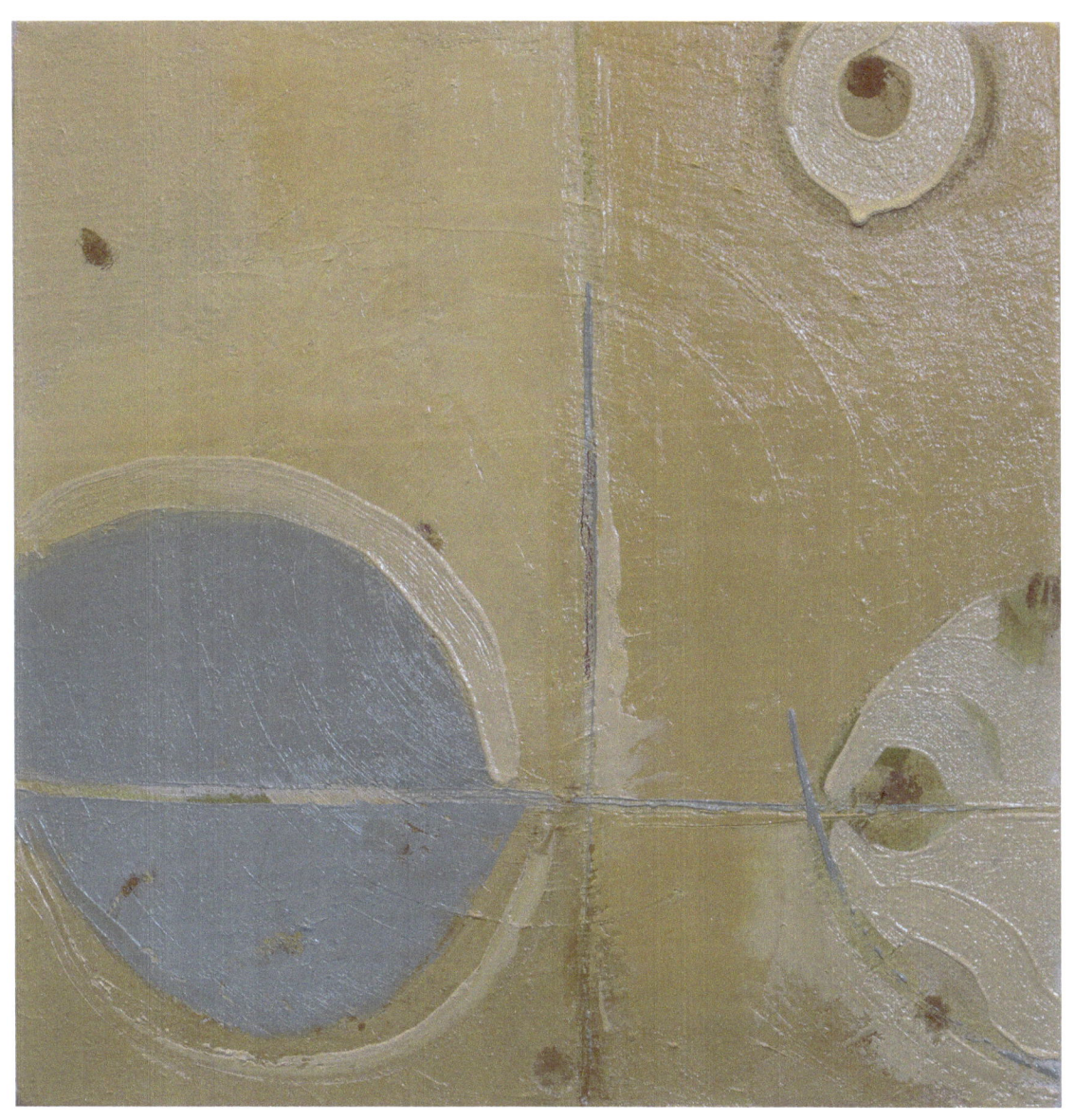

Katie Hawkinson  Budding Out  16″x16″ Oil on canvas  2013

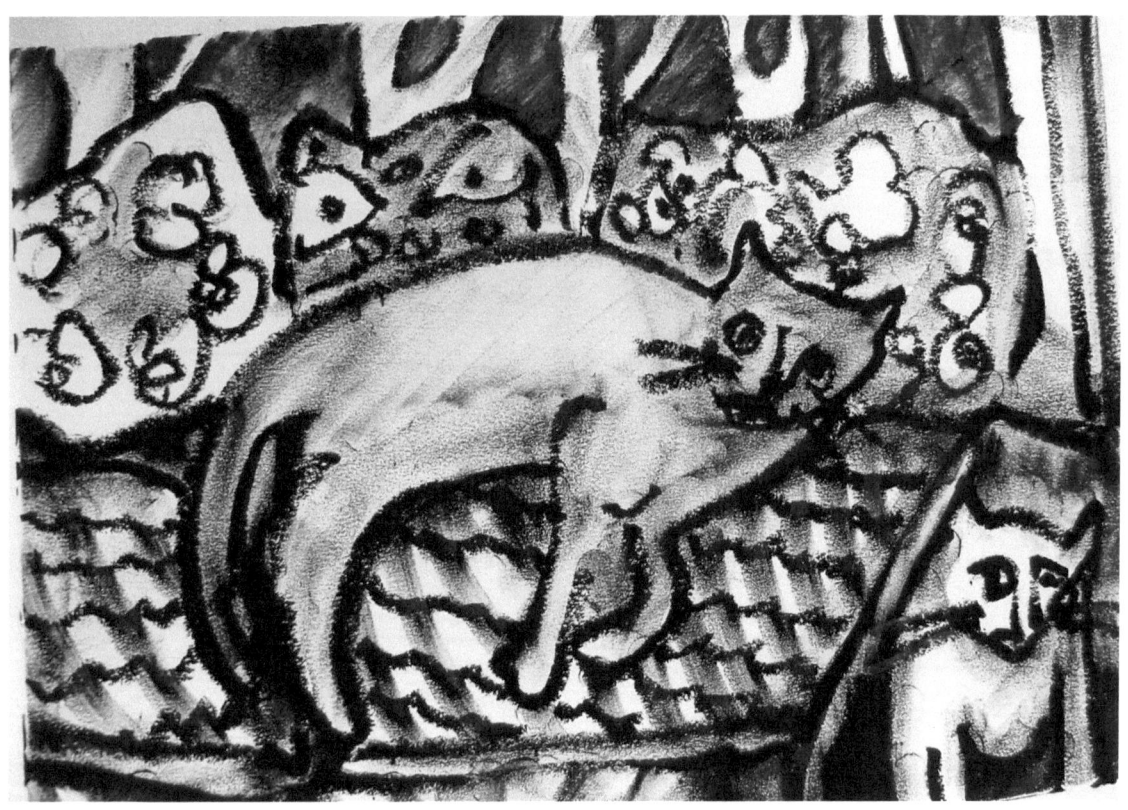

Barbara Hazard  Cat with Guardian  12″x18″  Oil pastel on paper  2002

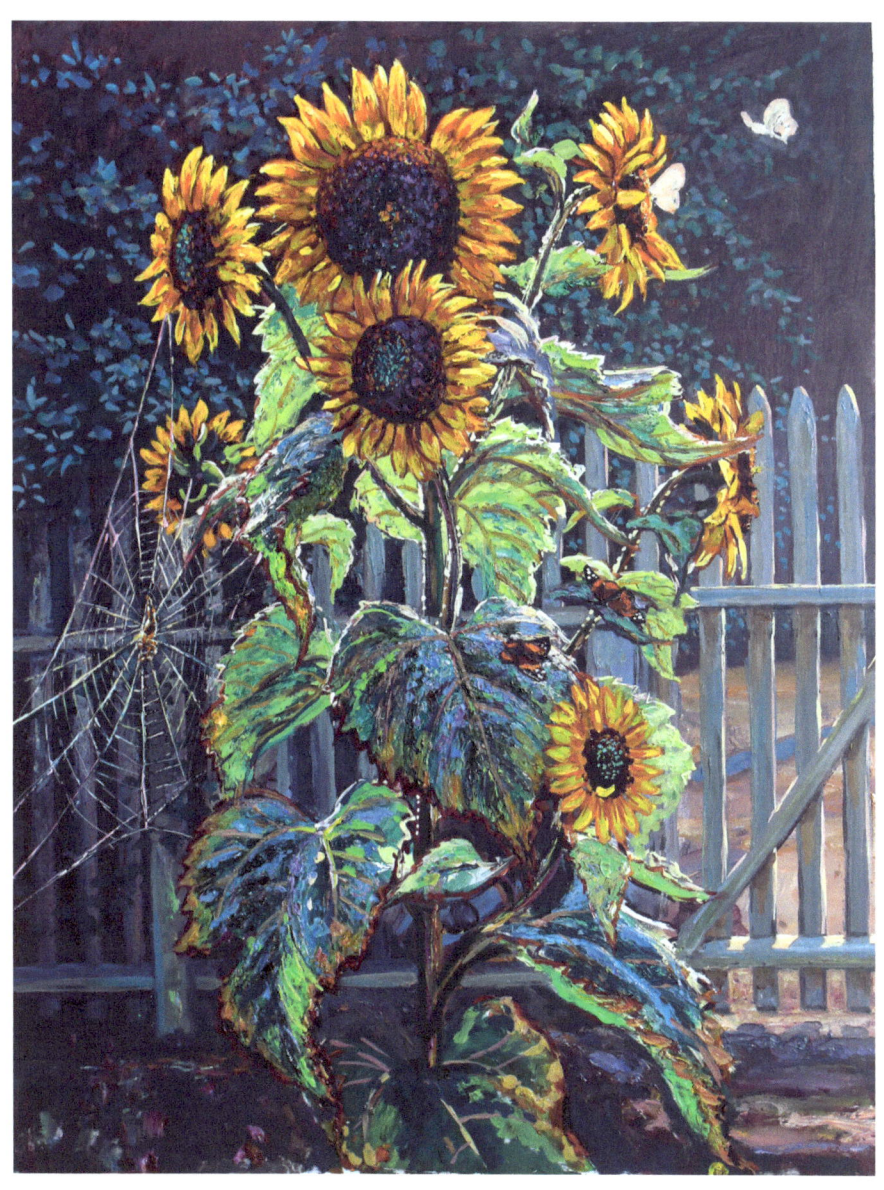

Anthony Holdsworth  September Sunflower  28″x20″  Oil on wood panel  2011

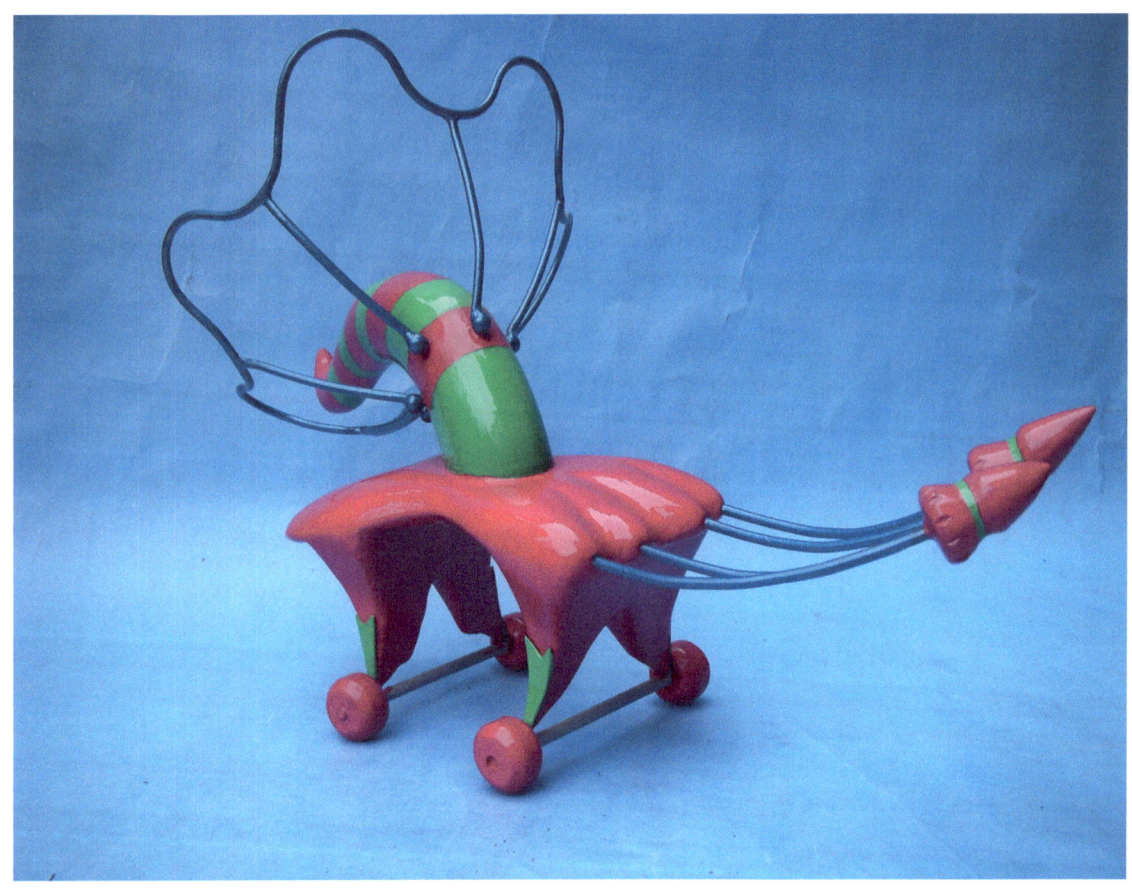

Stan Huncilman  Princess Perfect  14″(h)x20″(w)x10″(d)  Sculpture  2011

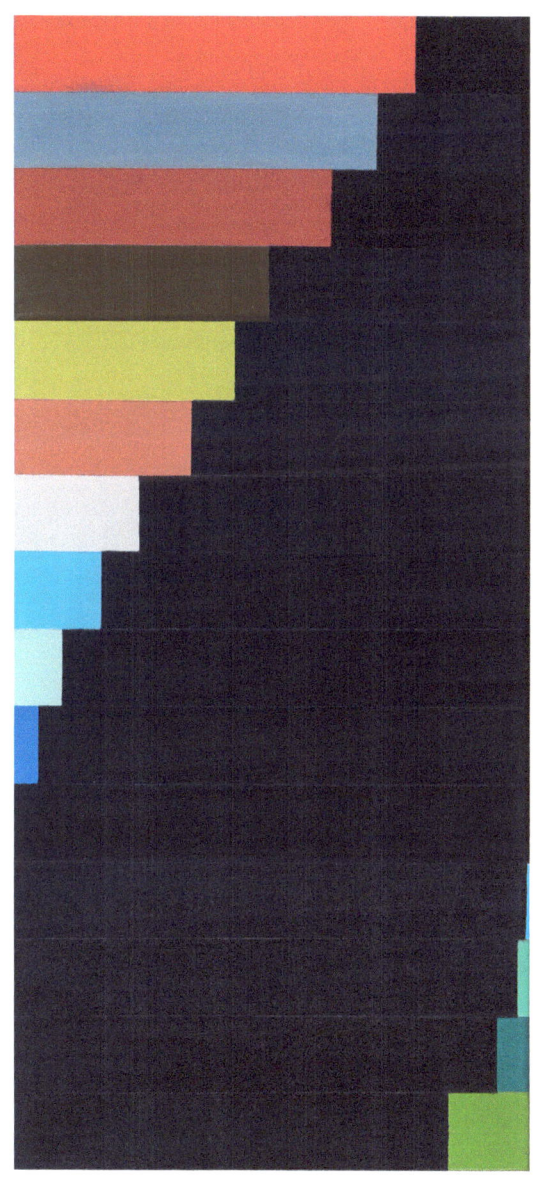

Carol Ladewig  Lunar Phases, Weeks 35, 36, 37, and 38(detail)  48″(h)x12″(w)x1.5″(d) panels(4- 12″x12″)
Acrylic/gouache on canvas  2012

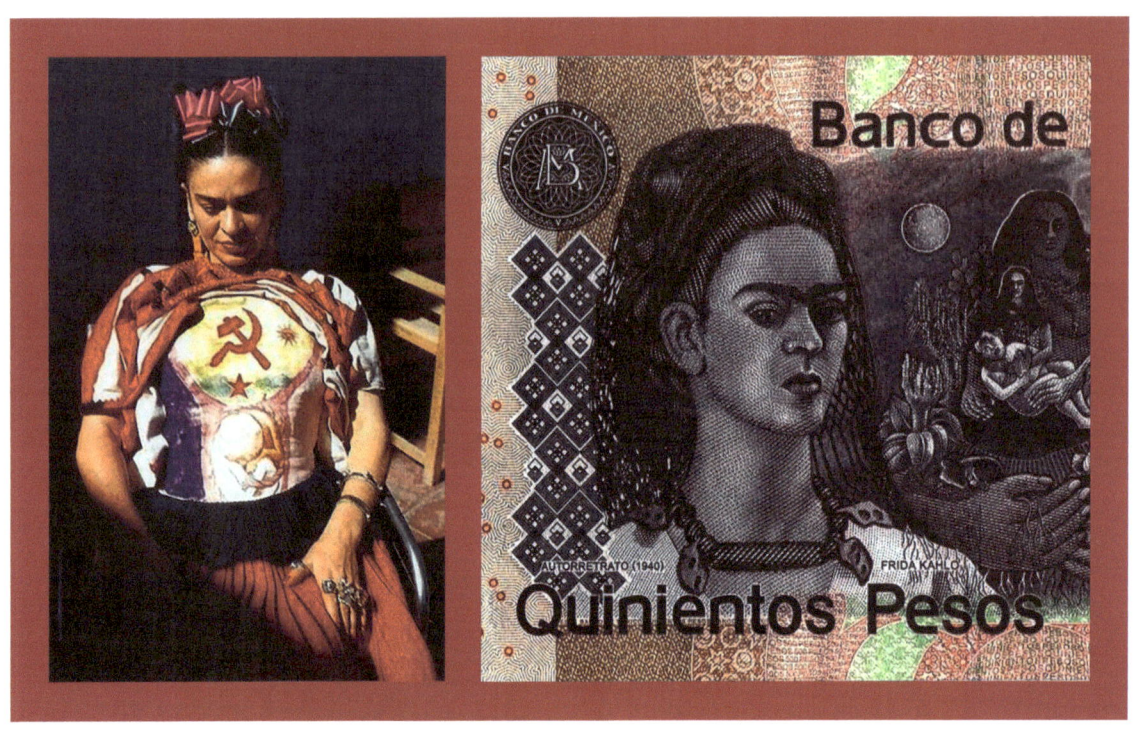

P.G. Meier  Quiniententos Pesos  11.5"x19"  Archival inkjet  2013

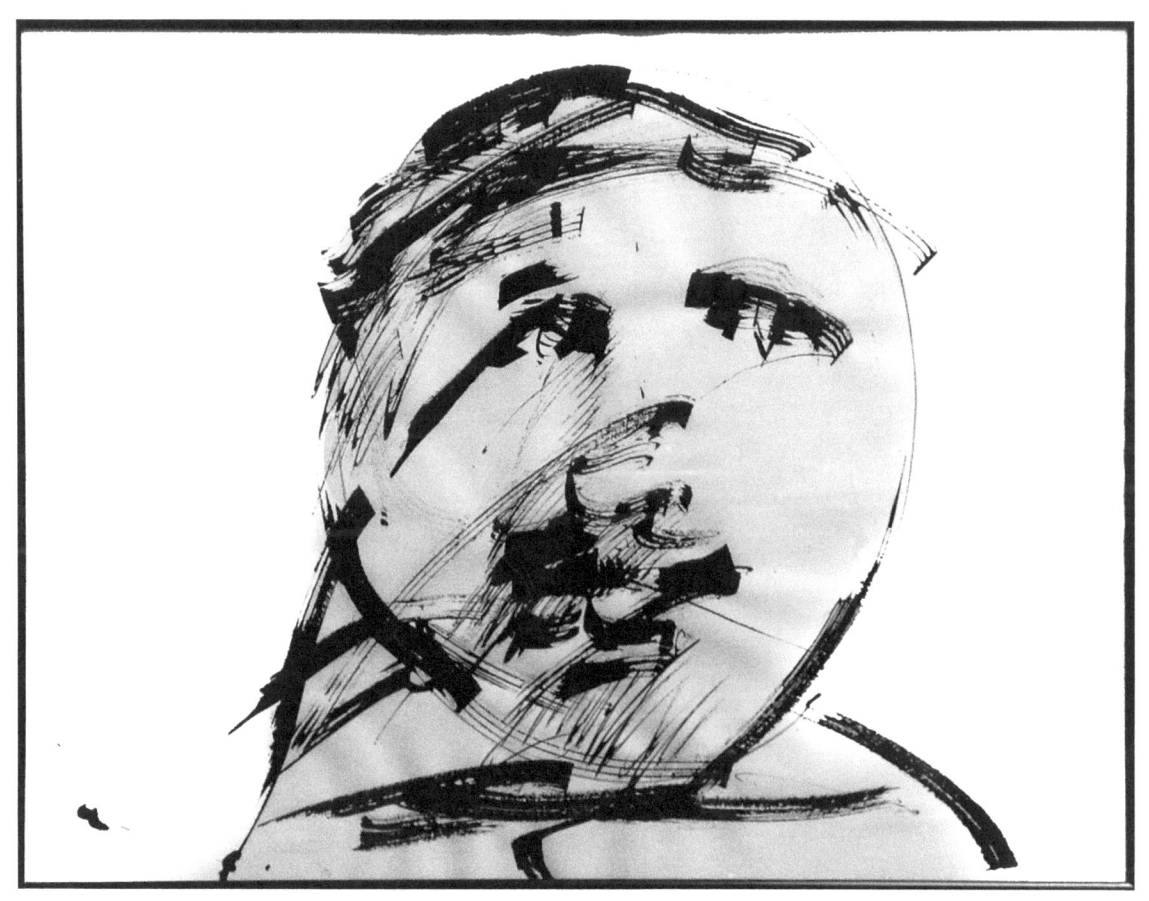

Arthur Monroe  Untitled  18″x24″  India ink drawing  1998

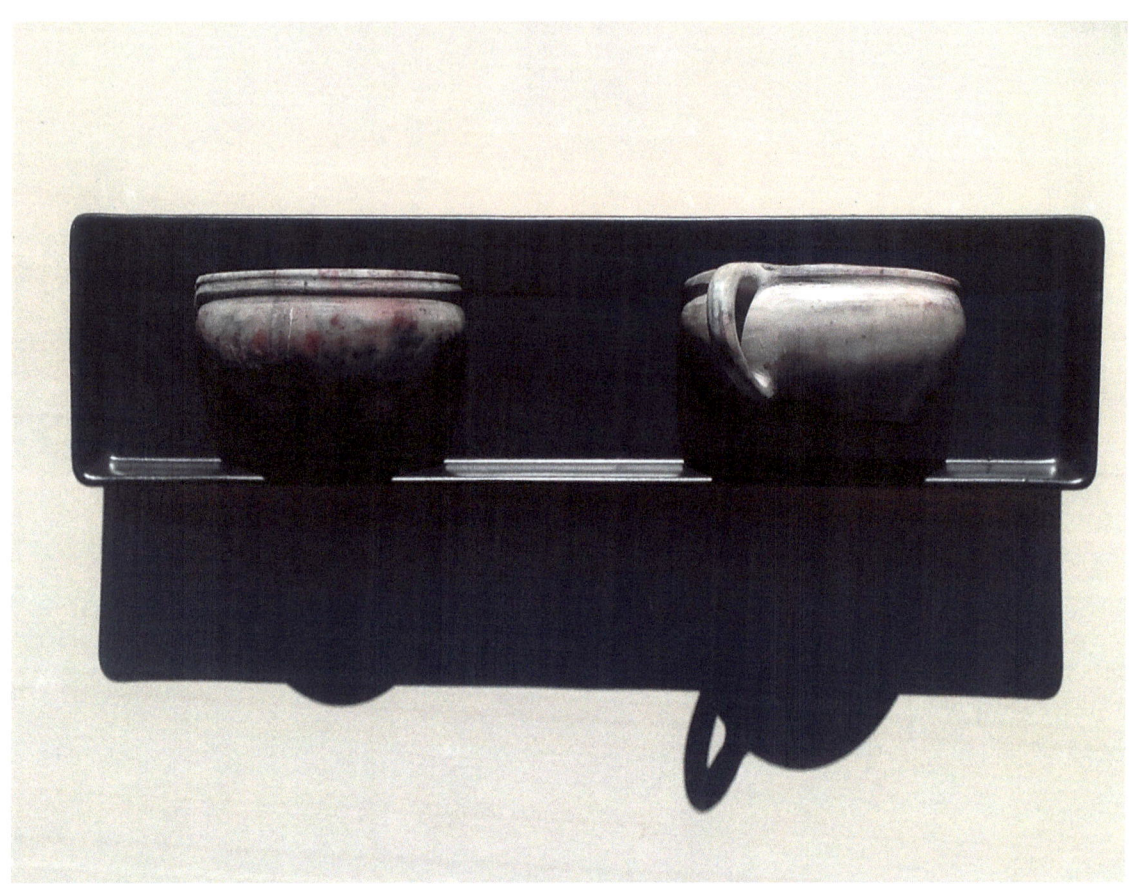

Guillermo Pulido  Naturaleza Muerta/Still Life  4.5″x17″  Ceramic wall relief sculpture  2013

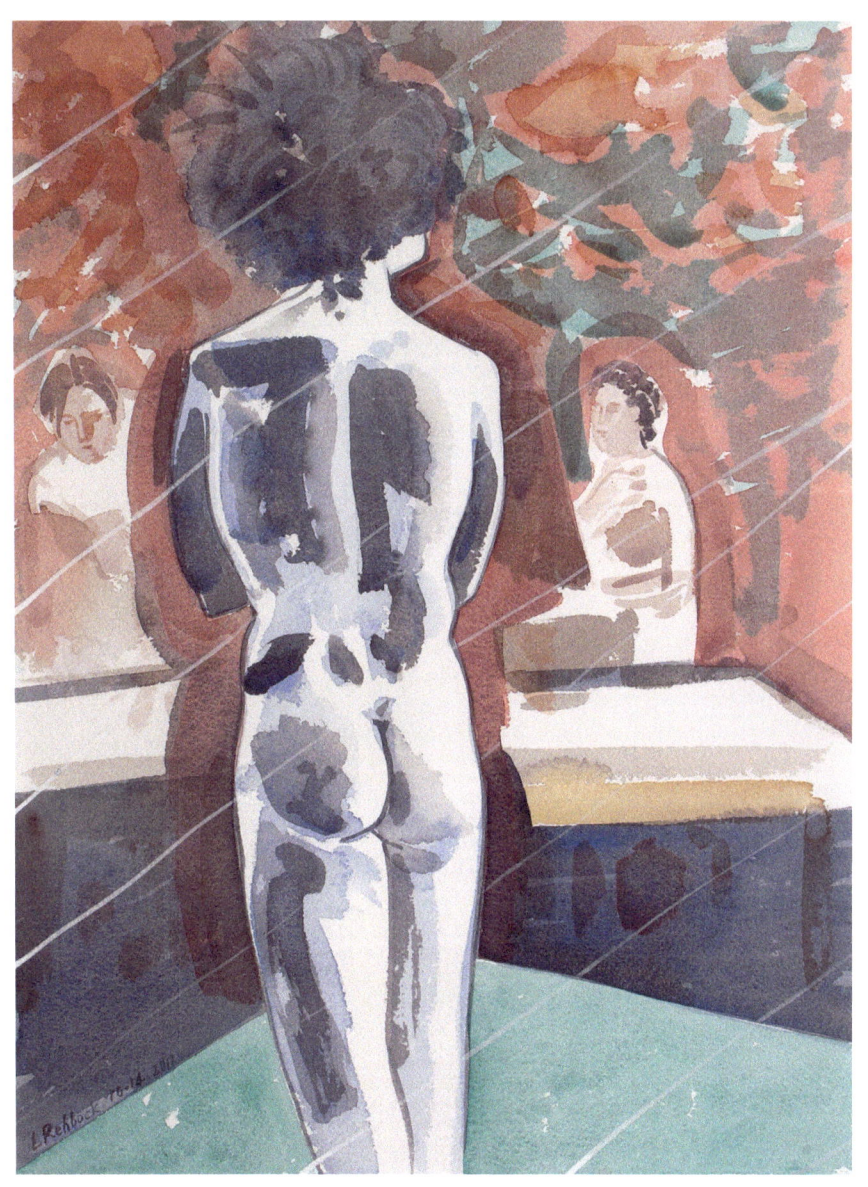

Loren Rehbock  Break Dancer III  16″x22″  Watercolor 2011

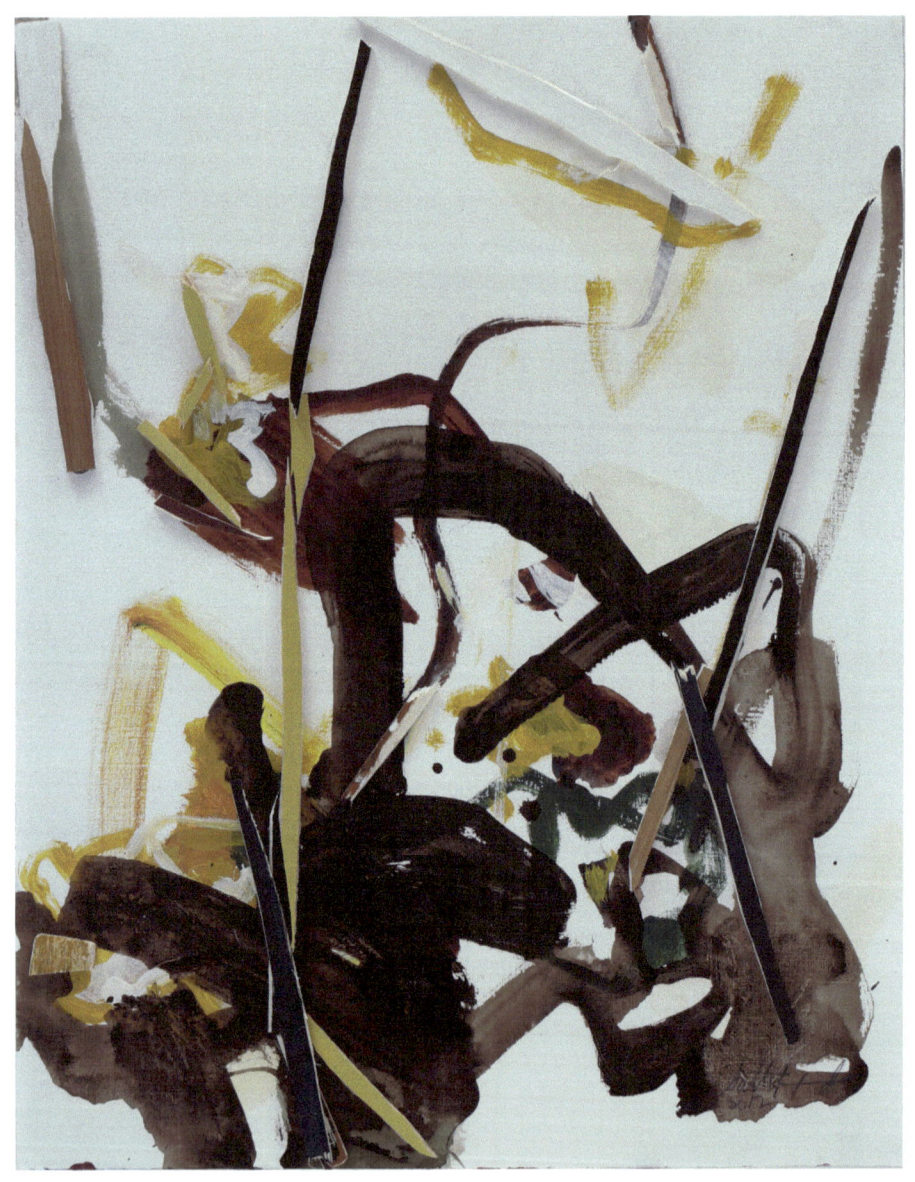

Foad Satterfield  Tangle  20"x24"  Acrylic, paint sticks on paper  2012

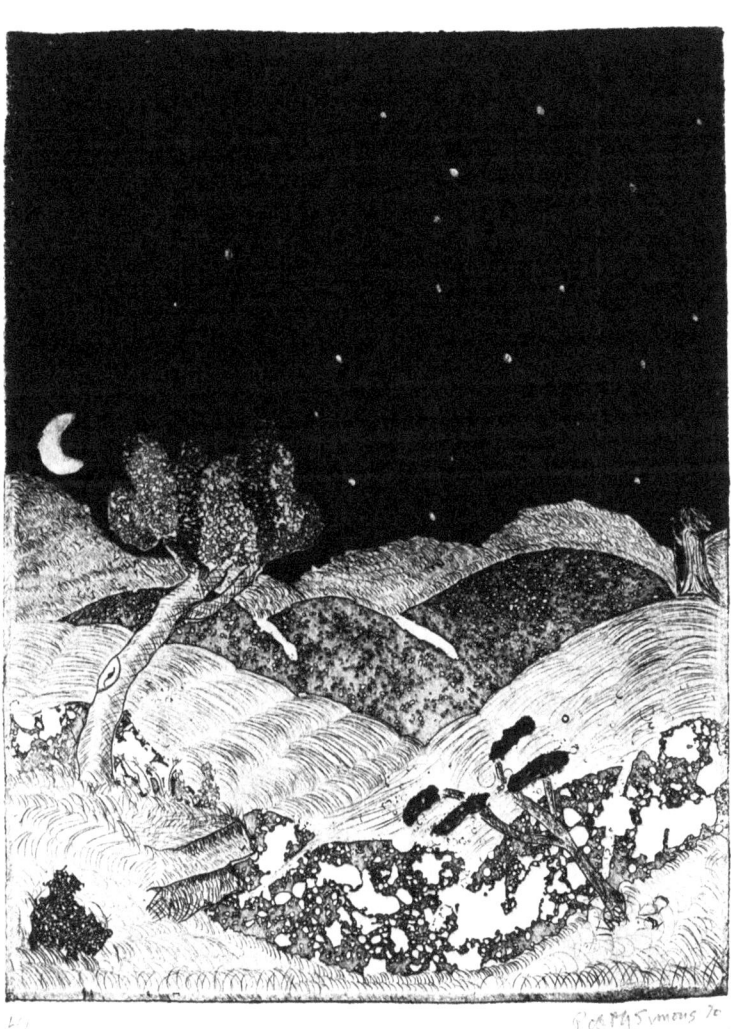

Robert Simons  Night Landscape Orinda   16x13″  Etching and aquatint  1970

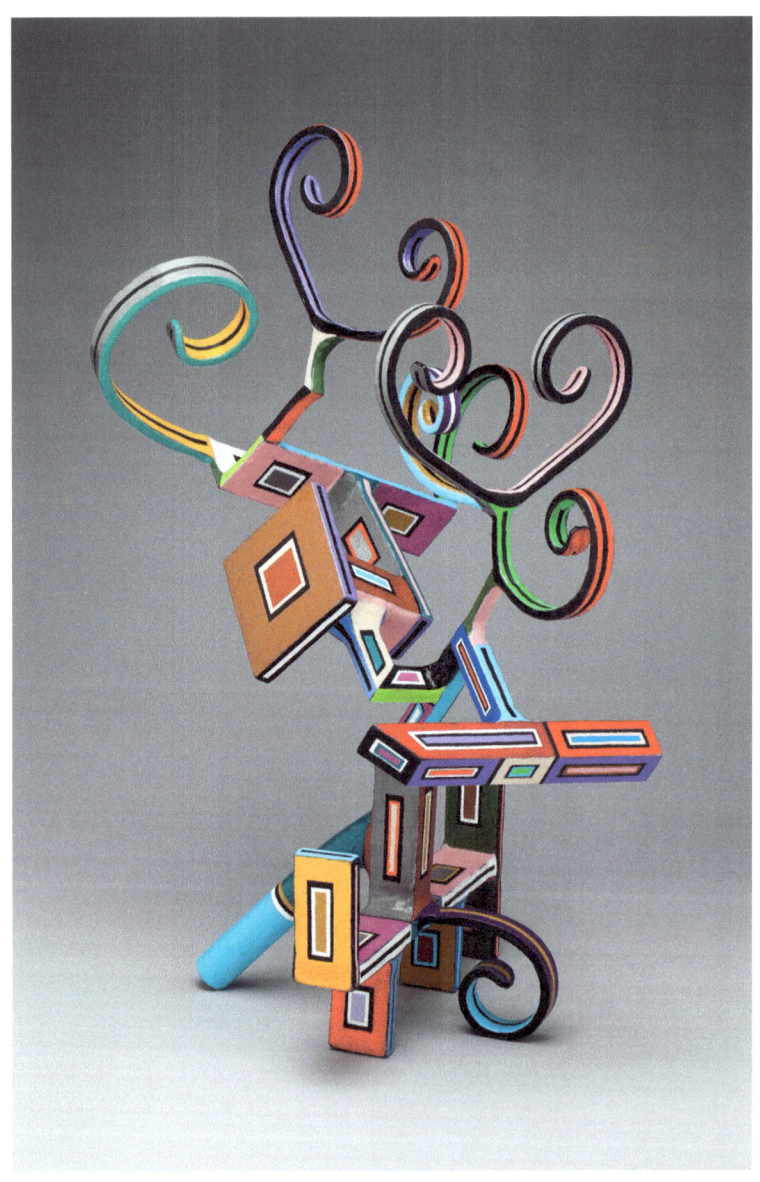

Joseph Slusky  Cakewalk  21″(h)x14″x(d)x13″(w)  Steel and acrylic laquer paint  2011

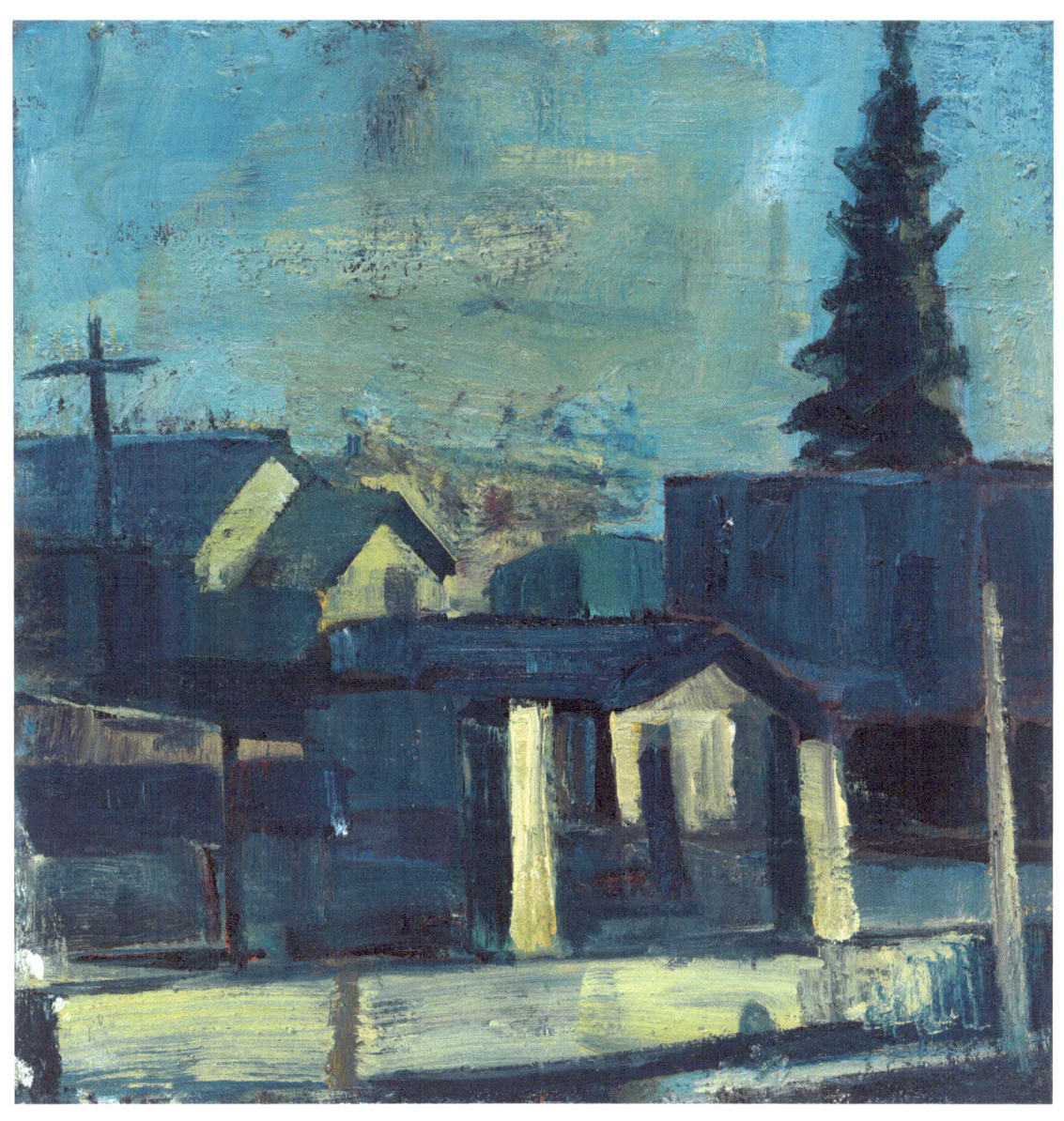

Terry St. John  Late Night Crockett  36"x36"  Oil on canvas  nd

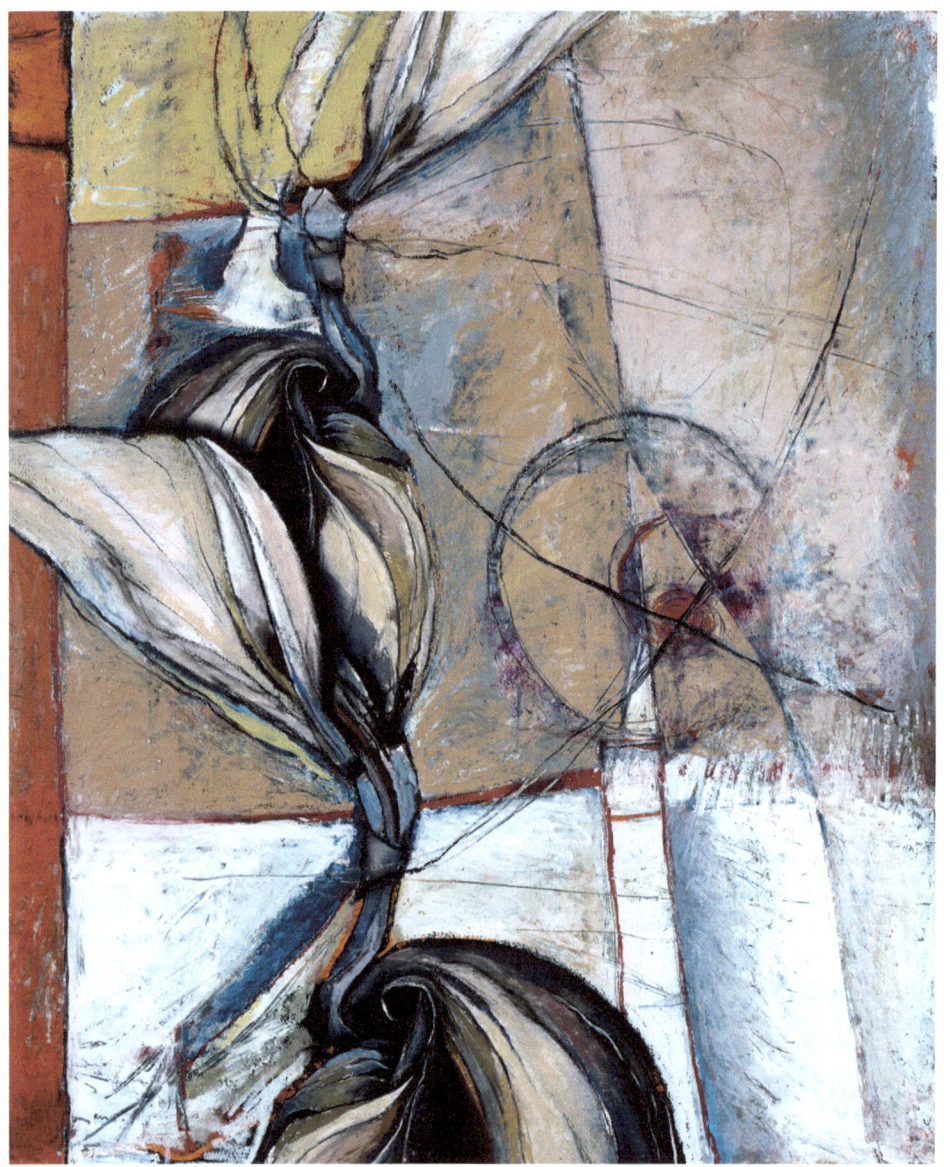

Kim Thoman  Iris Heart 6  22"x18"  Mixed media  2009

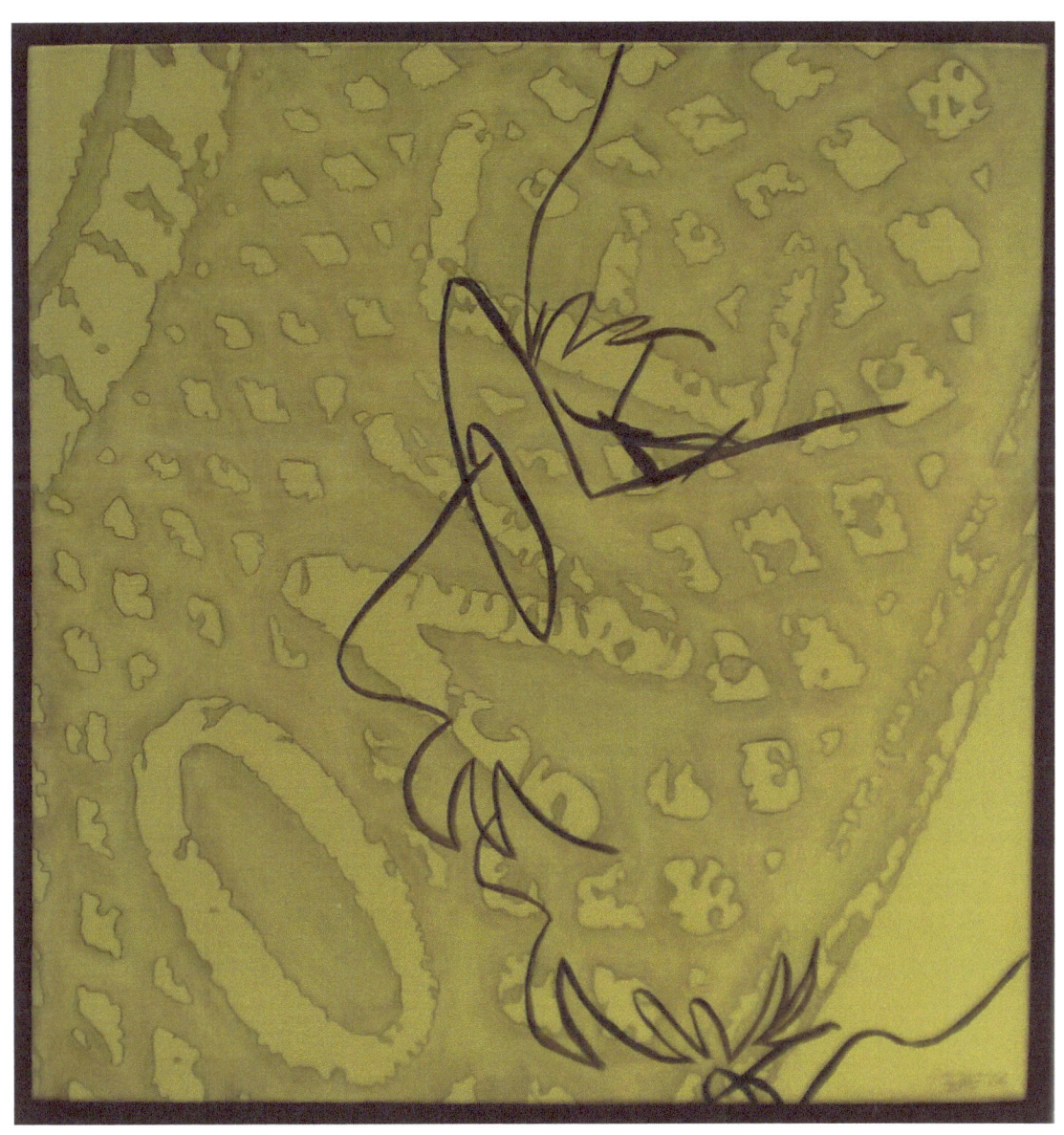

Genn Toffey   Subway Token Kyle   16"x16"   Mixed media on canvas  2010

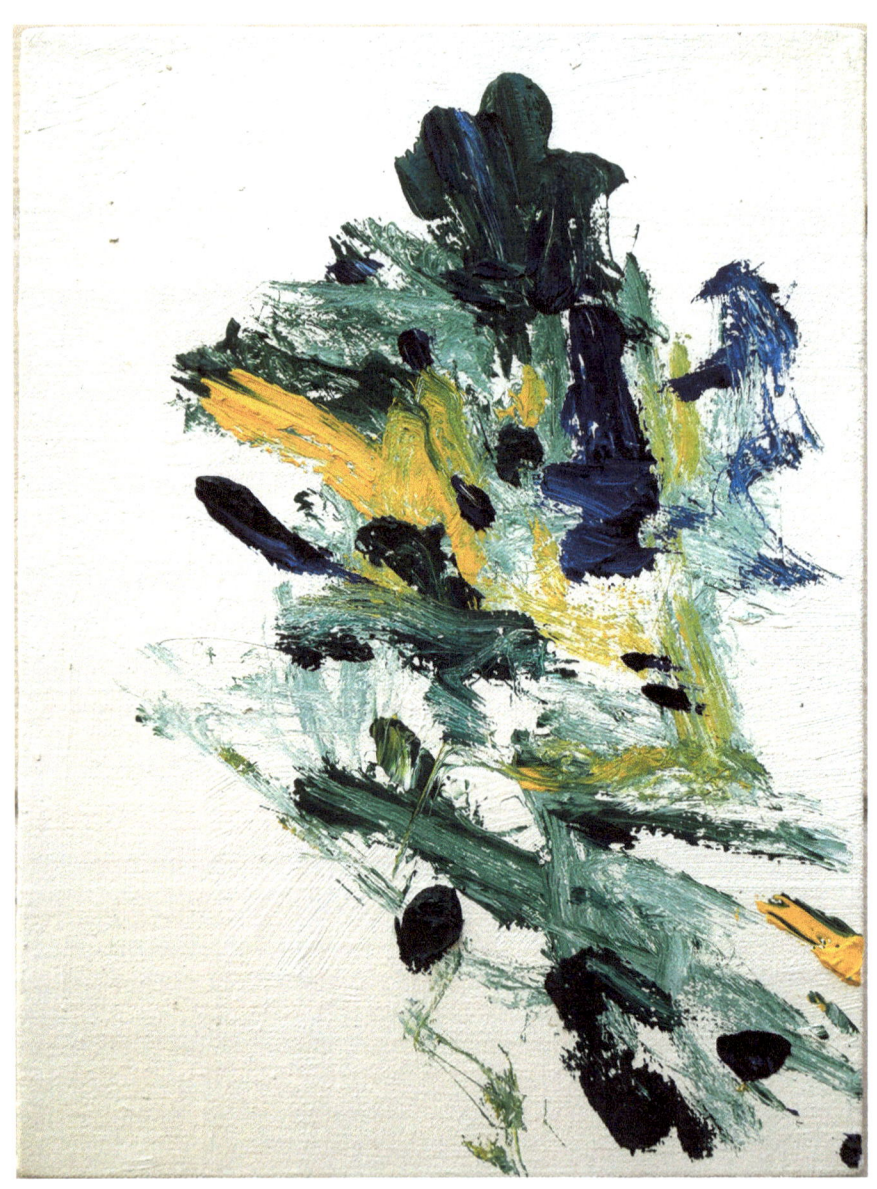

Sandy Walker   Etude 7   12″x9″  Oil on canvas  1997

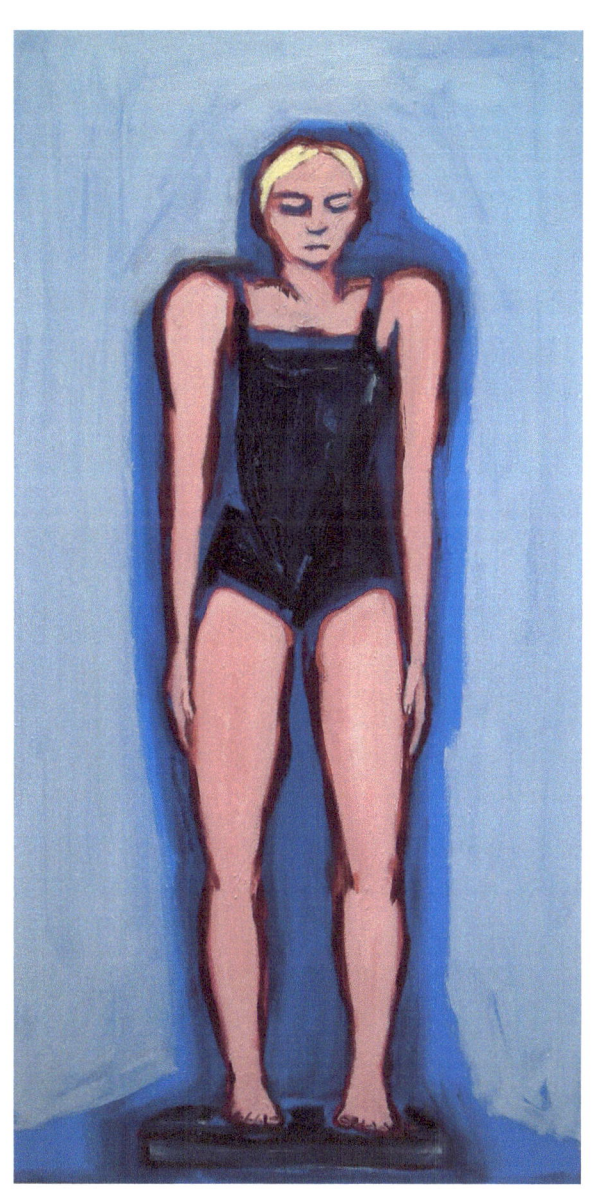

Jan Wurm   The Dive  36"x18"  Oil on canvas  2011

# The Breakfast Group at the Carl Cherry Center

November 1–December 15, 2013
4th and Guadalupe
Carmel, California

Edythe Bresnahan
Bruce Chaban
Donna Fenstermaker
Lin Fischer
John Friedman
Nancy Genn
Katie Hawkinson
Barbara Hazard
Anthony Holdsworth
Stan Huncilman
Carol Ladewig
P.G. Meier
Arthur Monroe
Guillermo Pulido
Loren Rehbock
Foad Satterfield
Robert Simons
Joseph Slusky
Terry St. John
Kim Thoman
Genn Toffey
Sandy Walker
Jan Wurm

www.ingramcontent.com/pod-product-compliance
Lightning Source LLC
Chambersburg PA
CBHW041301180526
45172CB00003B/922